NEW
HORIZONS

OXFORD

Christmas
SATB and organ

T0346916

—CECILIA McDOWALL—
A Christmas Carol

in memory of Hubert Dawkes

A Christmas Carol

G. K. Chesterton (1874–1936)

CECILIA McDOWALL

Duration: 3 mins

Printed in Great Britain

OXFORD UNIVERSITY PRESS, MUSIC DEPARTMENT, GREAT CLARENDON STREET, OXFORD OX2 6DP

are,_____ hearts__ are.)

are,_____ here the_ true hearts are.)

are,_____ true hearts__ are.)

are.)_____

The Christ - child lay on__

The Christ - child__ lay on

Ma - ry's__ heart, His hair was like a fire. (O__

Ma - ry's__ heart, His__ hair was like a fire.

His hair_____ was like__ a__ fire.__ (O__

His__ hair was like a fire. (O

The Christ - child stood at____ Ma - ry's____ knee, His

The Christ - child stood at____ Ma - ry's____ knee, His

The Christ - child stood at____ Ma - ry's____ knee, His

The Christ - child stood at____ Ma - ry's____ knee, His

Printed and bound in Great Britain by Caligraving Ltd, Thetford, Norfolk.

NEW HORIZONS showcases the wealth of exciting, innovative, and occasionally challenging choral music being written today. It encompasses the whole gamut of small-scale choral genres, both secular and sacred, and includes pieces for upper-voice and mixed choirs. With titles by some of the most accomplished choral composers active in the United Kingdom and abroad, the series introduces new repertoire and fresh talent to a broad spectrum of choirs.

Cecilia McDowall

Photo: Christie Dickason

Born in 1951 and educated at Edinburgh and London Universities, Cecilia McDowall has been described by the *International Record Review* as having a 'communicative gift that is very rare in modern music'. An award-winning composer, McDowall is often inspired by extra-musical influences, and her choral writing combines rhythmic vitality with expressive lyricism. Her music has been commissioned, performed, and recorded by leading choirs, among them Phoenix Chorale and the Choir of New College, Oxford, and is regularly programmed at prestigious festivals in Britain and abroad.

NH260   **A Christmas Carol**   McDOWALL

OXFORD
UNIVERSITY PRESS

www.oup.com

ISBN 978-0-19-355161-9

9 780193 551619